God Made Me

God Made Me, UK English edition

© C.R. Draper, 2019

Illustrations and cover design by Nadia Rajput

All rights reserved. No part of this book may be reproduced in any form or by any electronic or mechanical means, without permission in writing from the copyright owner.

ISBN: 978-1-909986-47-3

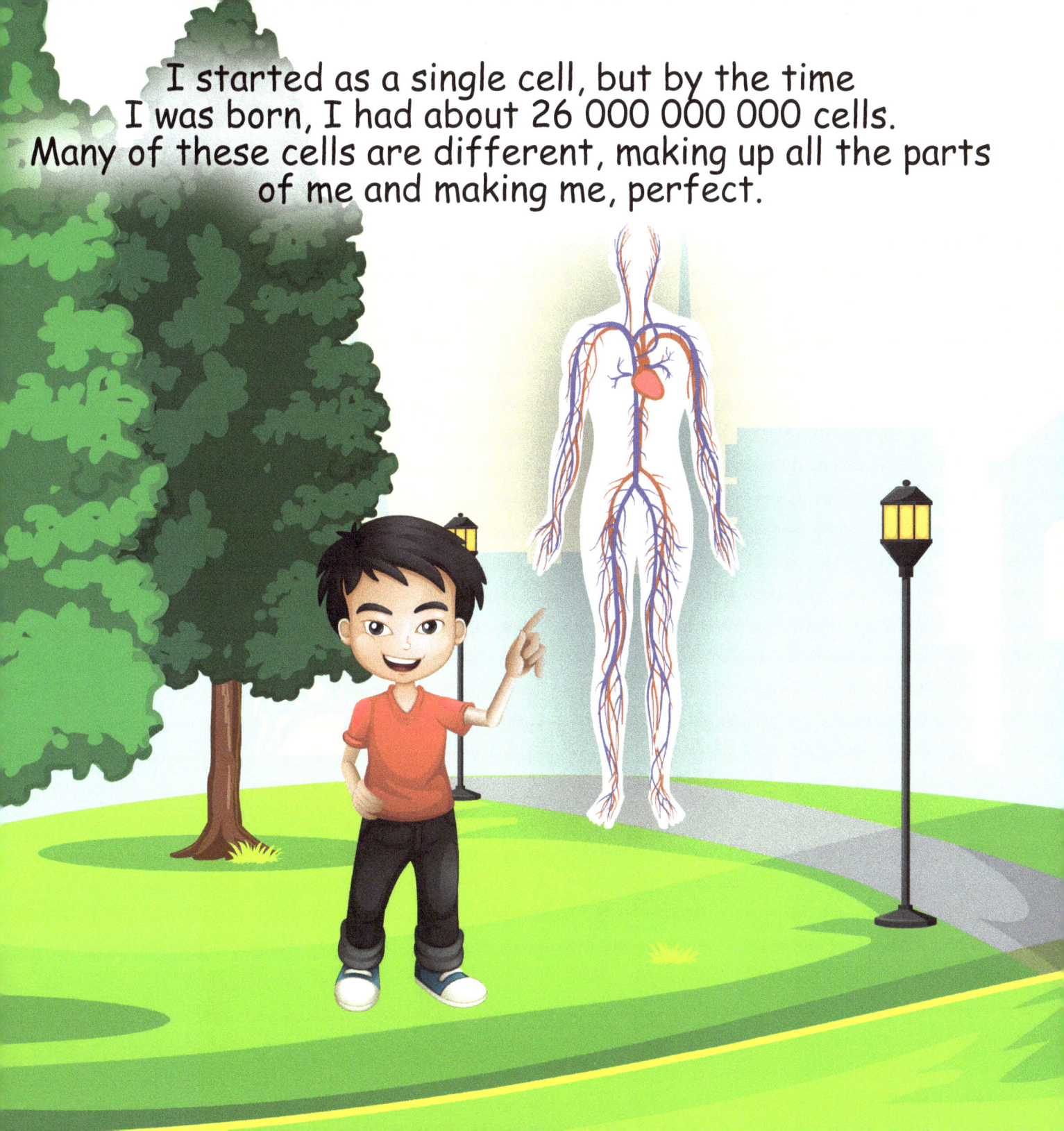

I started as a single cell, but by the time I was born, I had about 26 000 000 000 cells. Many of these cells are different, making up all the parts of me and making me, perfect.

My heart pumps blood around 100 000 km of blood vessels. Enough to go around the world twice.

God made my lungs to breathe. The air sacs in my lungs, when stretched out, would fill a tennis court. This allows me to breathe in 11 000 litres of air, every day. That's about 70 bathtubs full of air.

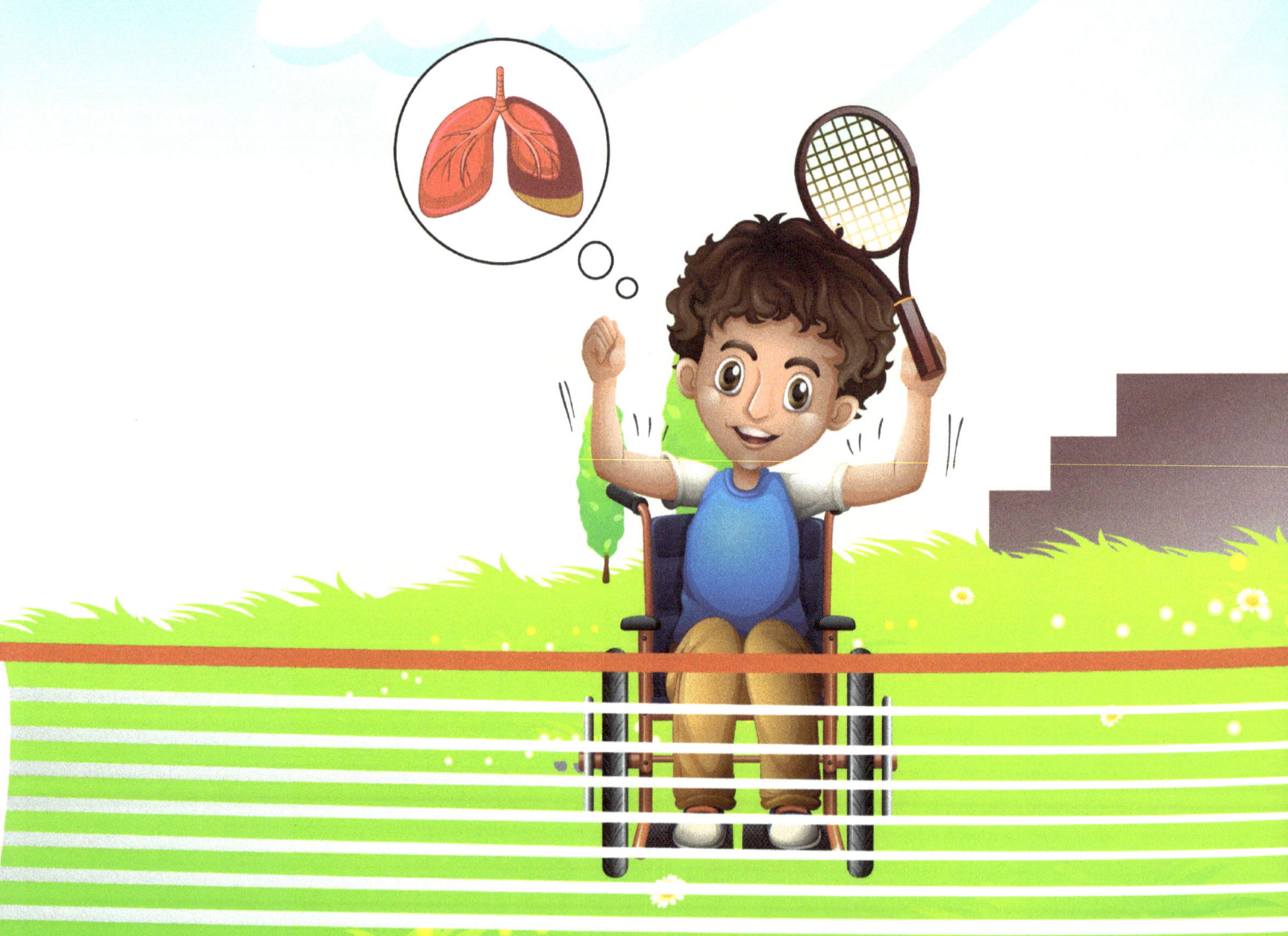

The oxygen that I take in combines with sugar to make energy, energy for my heart to beat and my mouth to sing.

The tongue is the only muscle in the body that does not work with any support from our bones. It is a strong muscle. God made our tongue strong; it can bring love and encouragement or hurt and tears. We need to use our tongue wisely.

Besides talking, I use my mouth to eat. It produces a litre of saliva every day and chops up my food with my teeth.

Of those 206 bones, 56 are in the wrist and hands. This means I can write, use a phone, play the piano and use my hands to serve others.

My bones are very strong, they are even stronger than concrete. The thigh bone, called the femur, is the longest bone and the strongest.

Not all bones are as big as the thigh bone. The bone in my inner ear, called the stirrup, is the smallest bone. It is only two to three millimetres long, even in adults, like my parents.

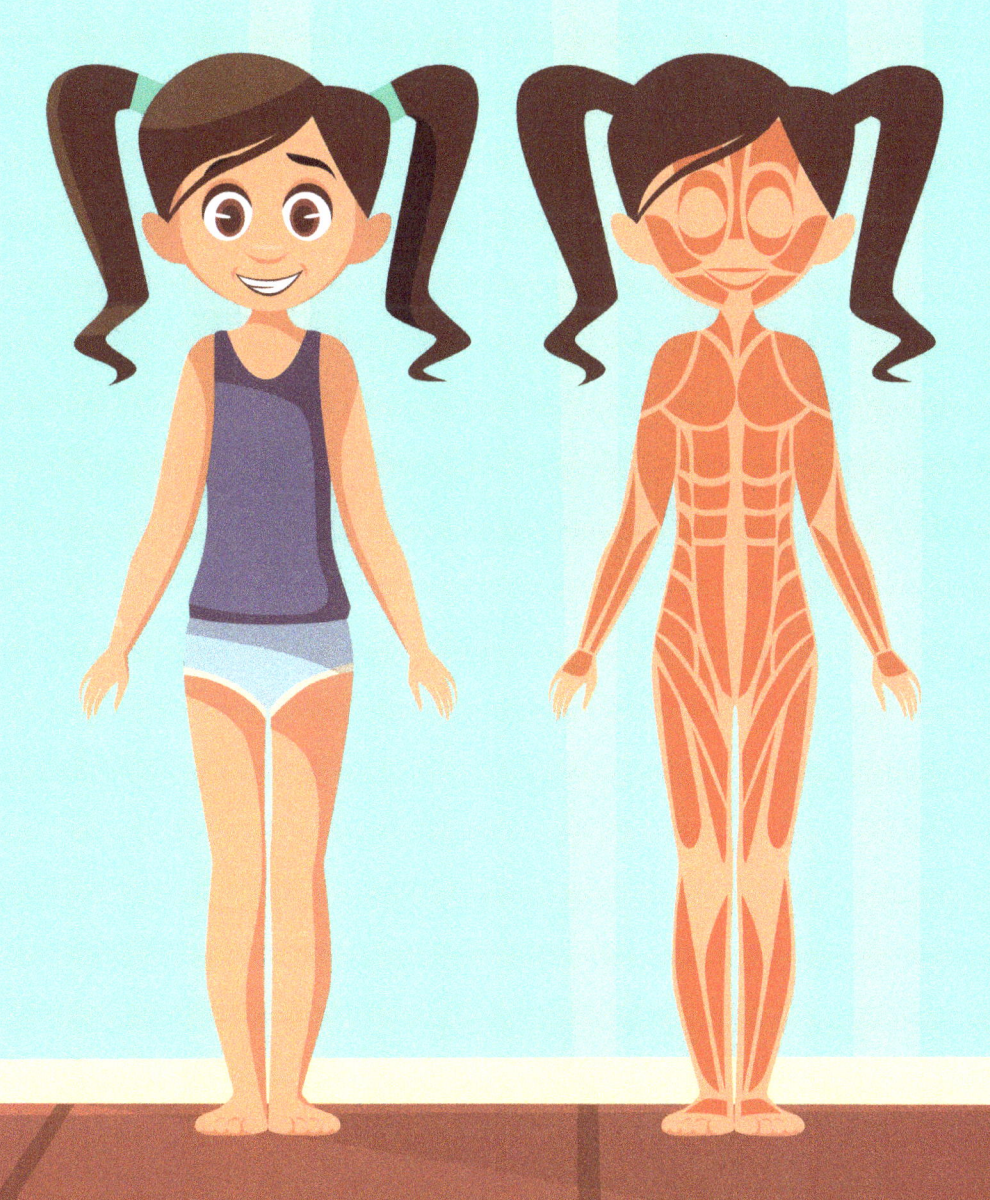

Muscles are attached to my bones.
Muscles pull, but they cannot push.

If all the nerve cells in my body were lined up, they would be 965 km long. That is a very big communication system.

My body is complex, but it is truly amazing. God made my body different from everyone else, it is wonderfully and perfectly made.

God made me to fulfil a part of His plan, a part just for me.
Thank you, God.

www.ingramcontent.com/pod-product-compliance
Lightning Source LLC
Chambersburg PA
CBHW042032100526
44587CB00029B/4394